*Praise for* **Imagine**

*"Sandy's book,* ***Imagine****, hits the spot for anyone on the roaa towards unearthing their limitless potential. Her knowledge and teachings about paradigms and shifting is a testament to how we all need to live in the "now." Detours certainly come up in our lives, which assist with self discovery and implementing personal boundaries, which help us to make the best of our biggest commodity; time. Imagine is a wonderful practice book with anecdotes from Sandy's own personal life, which certainly paves the way in reminding us, that in the end, we are all human. This is a must-read for anyone looking to make a conscious shift in their thinking. Thoughts are actions, and Sandy reminds us that we have the power to do and be what our heart desires. Thank you for writing this book Sandy, your teachings are universal."*

Pashmina P., International bestselling author of *The Cappuccino Chronicles* Trilogy

*"****Imagine, Navigating without Life's GPS*** *is a book that will take you on a journey of discovering that everything you have learned in life has prepared you for your destiny. Sandy takes you to a point in your life when you should reclaim using your imagination, vision and senses to dream again, just as you did when you were a child. Believe in yourself. Fasten your virtual seat belts and allow your Imagination to navigate you."*

Judy O'Beirn, founder and co-author of International Bestselling *Unwavering Strength* book series

# IMAGINE

## NAVIGATING WITHOUT LIFE'S GPS

SANDY FORSEILLE

Published by Hasmark Publishing
www.hasmarkpublishing.com


First Edition



Disclaimer

This book is designed to provide information and motivation to our readers. It is sold with the understanding that the publisher is not engaged to render any type of psychological, legal, or any other kind of professional advice. The content of each article is the sole expression and opinion of its author, and not necessarily that of the publisher. No warranties or guarantees are expressed or implied by the publisher's choice to include any of the content in this volume. Neither the publisher nor the individual author(s) shall be liable for any physical, psychological, emotional, financial, or commercial damages, including, but not limited to, special, incidental, consequential or other damages. Our views and rights are the same: You are responsible for your own choices, actions, and results.

Permission should be addressed in writing to Sandy Forseille at sandy.forseille@gmail.com

Editor: Corinne Casazza
corinnecasazza@gmail.com

Cover & Book Design: Anne Karklins
anne@hasmarkpublishing.com

ISBN 13: 978-1-989161-87-6
ISBN 10: 1989161871

*This book is dedicated to all the teachers who've devoted their time and effort to learning transformational information and helping others change their lives. Along this journey I've learned as parents we're responsible for our children's paradigms, and I am the only one responsible for changing mine. I can allow myself to accept and respond to any situation. I can take control of my life and achieve the results I desire.*

*Thank you, Thank you and Thank you.*

# Table of Contents

# Acknowledgments

Never stop using your imagination. Believe in yourself and your dreams will come true. If you have failures, hold your head up and stand up tall. This is where the new you is growing your wings to fly.

To all the people who ever came into my life and allowed me to come into yours. It is no accident why we crossed paths, but I will be forever grateful that we have.

To my family for pushing me off the cliff, and to my parents for giving me the tools to climb back up, showing me the person to be; not who anyone thinks I should be.

I want to thank my three musketeers: Auntie Marilyn, Auntie Marie and my friend Tab. The three of you gave me the words of wisdom and encouragement to keep persevering even when I needed a kick in the butt to finish this book.

Thank you to all the people who gave me the chance to see Christmas through a child's eyes. Every time I decorate my trees you are there with me. When the lights are twinkling, I know you're sending me your love.

Thank you to Kevin Dutchak for your support and believing in me when my book was complete. I pray this book gives you encouragement and love. I hope your caring for others and your son Ryan proves to you you're a special man. I hope you can see the results of your actions in the people you touch.

Thank you to my late mother-in-law Lulu who always gave me that hug and shared her faith about letting God take the wheel, showing me that God will be there in the calm waters and the roughest storms.

Thank you to my beautiful daughters. I am so proud to have the gift of being your mom. I carried you both in my womb for nine months and under my wing for your early years. I watched you both come out from that cocoon of childhood to becoming "women, wives and mothers. It has been a blessing to become your friend. You both have taught me so much compassion and inspiration in your life's challenges, and I know that God is there for your calm waters and storms too. Don't ever stop the gift of dreaming; keep your imagination alive. Smile at your failures because you know growth is right there at your fingertips. Thank you to your husbands, Stefan and Wes, for being on this journey.

I want to thank Danny for being my friend and for all the growth we've experienced together. You were there through sickness and health, and you have been my rock. Thank you for allowing me to call you at 2 am when I woke up with a new idea for my book. You never got upset. Thank you for never shaking your head when I put up the fifth, sixth and seventh. Christmas trees. Instead, you just smiled and said, "they look nice." Thank you for allowing me to live that little girl's dream. You supported me through all the adventures we went on.

To my grandchildren, who are the light of my world. I love you all so much. Faith, Hope, Dion, Wesley, Kyndre and Taylah. I am so blessed to be your nana and have your unconditional love. You make me smile, you make me laugh, you give me that hug when I didn't even realize that I needed it. Just the words "I Love you Nana" melt my heart and show me life's purpose. Always use that inner child's imagination and playfulness. Be like Peter Pan and believe.

# Introduction

When I grow up, I'm going to be just like you. Think back to when you were a child. How many times you would say to yourself or others, "When I grow up I'm going to be Cinderella or Superman, maybe the bionic woman or bionic man. I remember playing with my friends and we would act and imitate that person we admired. I can envision my friends and I pretending to be like Cinderella sipping on tea at tea parties, we could even imagine tasting the flavor of the tea, smelling the perfume of our Mother's or grandmothers as we sprinkled it on ourselves. We dressed up in our mother's scarves and wore her high heels trying to walk and speak gracefully. We spent time looking in the mirror at ourselves with lipstick on and danced around. We were Cinderella as far as we were concerned. If we were the bionic woman or superman, we'd pretend to pick up heavy objects. They were really light, but in our imagination we could see the boulder, feel the weight, and even hear the music when pretending to run in slow motion just like our idles could.

We were that person in our minds because we wanted to be that person we saw on television or read about in a book. Later in life we started looking around at the people in our lives and realized that maybe when we grew up, we wanted to be like them. Maybe we wanted to be a doctor because we witnessed one helping people, and we understood how great it feels to make people healthy. We thought of being a teacher because we loved our teachers. They taught us to read and write; they spent extra with us because we were struggling and they gave us confidence in our abilities.

Do you have a fireman or truck driver in your family? I was surrounded by truck drivers, and I was the only girl with four brothers. We'd play trucks and pretend we were working with our dad driving truck. I remember making engine noises of pretending to go up a hill or coming to a stop. Do you ever stop and wonder how we knew to use our senses and imaginations?

Growing up we just learn and imagine and role play being someone else, but how do we really know those things? It wasn't until two years ago when I decided to take a program that it all made sense, just like putting a puzzle together. I was introduced to this program by a woman who took my air brakes course for semi-trucks. After the air brakes course she was telling me about this program that her friend facilitated and how it changed her way of thinking. She said she changed the results in her life. Because I loved to teach and talk, she'd thought I'd enjoy the program. I signed up and also completed the certified program to facilitate it.

I discovered everything you've done and learned in life, every life lesson, every new adventure, every person who's entered your life even for a short time, has prepared you for reaching your destination. You were on these people's paths for a reason. Failures in life weren't really failures. They were lessons; probably the best life lessons you'll ever have. I know they were for me. My failures were where I learned the most. They made me who I am today and I wouldn't change any road I've been down because they've made me the person I am today.

I've done many jobs and have taken many courses through the years. Some people criticized me because they didn't understand, but now I can stand straight and be proud of every road that I've travelled. I'm so grateful that you have decided to take this road trip with me and I pray that you'll learn more about yourself as I did, with every road sign that appeared along my journey. This book has taken me back to teach me how to use my imagination, vision and senses to dream again just like that child so many years ago. The funny thing is everything is always right in front of us, we just have to go out and get it, open our imagination, believe in ourselves and trust that when situations or people cross our path it's for a reason or lesson. We can accept it or reject it.

Our imagination can be used positively or negatively. If we feel that vibration in our body is it a good vibration or bad? The great gift is we have is the ability to change it. We're in control of it. If we're in a negative state, we have to realize how we arrived there and know how to change it; we have to become aware. We have the capability to imagine ourselves in a **different job, place or situation**. We have to imagine the feeling of already achieving it. I am claustrophobic and when I had an MRI, I just lay there and imagined being on a beach, listening to the waves, feeling the sun, or I imagined myself at a seminar talking to people and reciting to myself what I'd be talking about. It does work.

*Fasten your seat belts and let's go for a road trip together.*

CHAPTER ONE

# Decision

Before we begin our road trip, we have to decide on a destination. Choosing a destination is like determining a goal, they have similar questions to ask ourselves to make the plan. Before we decide our destination, we have to be able to use our imagination just like we did when we were children and pretended to be our idol. As children we loved to hear people tell bedtime stories. I'm going to tell you stories about my life along the roads I've been on, not realizing the journey was leading me to become who I am today.

Opening up our imagination allows us to visualize and use our senses to believe that our goals or destination can be reached.

There are three types of goals:

**C Type** – This goal is a fantasy because you've never achieved it before. The goal should make you scared and excited at the same time. Do you really have the desire to do it and the feeling? Feelings are an emotions. These lead to actions which bring your results.

**B Type** – You think you can achieve this. You have the information, map and know-how.

**A Type** – You know you can accomplish this because you've done it before.

When choosing a destination, we can use the same three choices. We can plan an "A" type goal and go to the same place we always have and do the same things that make us feel safe and comfortable. Or we can choose a "B" type goal. We'll go somewhere different, but get all our ideas from others who've been there and done the exploring. We'll just follow their lead. Or, finally, we can plan a "C" type goal and just wing it. We'll choose a destination not knowing what we'll see along the way, but when we arrive we'll have learned a lot, and more importantly we'll have grown.

For our journey, we've decided on a "C" type destination. I'm so excited because it's going to be an adventure. Let's take our journals so we can write down what our experiences every day. As we begin to write in our journals, I'm going to write in the front what I'm happy and grateful for before we begin. I'm happy and grateful that I'll be traveling with someone who's on the same frequency as I am, we both have the same goals. We both feel the vibration of being adventurous. Next we have to plan what we're bringing with us. On this trip we have two pieces of luggage. One we'll open and the other will be in the trunk, we'll try not to open that one too often. At the end of this trip, I'll put the that bag and in the closet without removing the items. The following items: (OUR PARADIGMS)

**LUGGAGE ONE**
**Paradigms**

| | |
|---|---|
| Fear/worry | Anxiety |
| Doubt | Attitude |

**LUGGAGE TWO**
**Paradigms**

| | | |
|---|---|---|
| Attitude | Courage/Confidence | Forgiveness |
| Understanding | Gratitude | Joy |
| Faith/Trust | Compromise | Balance |
| Acceleration/Growth | Success | LOVE |
| Health/Wealth | Self-Worth | |

You might have noticed that there are a few words that are repeated. That's because paradigms are positive and negative. Repetition teaches us to control our paradigms. Let's put our baggage in the vehicle, put our sunglasses on and fasten our seat belts.

If you look back on your life, are there some roads you've travelled and wondered what the lesson was?

Do you ever look back at some choices you made and thought if I had gone down the other road, what would my life be like?

Who did you imagine you were as a child while playing? Who did you imagine you'd be when you grew up?

Whose influence helped you decide your future?

Can you imagine your luggage in your trunk; is it similar to mine?

What types of goals have you planned?

There are some things we have to remember to get the results we want:

1. **Just do it** – Stop making excuses. Get focused on the vision and discipline yourself to start practicing that focus. Get

excited about living the life you desire, you have to want it and really, really live that goal already. Get in tune with that frequency.

2. **Remember no one knows what we're capable of.** Sometimes we have to sit down and have a heart to heart talk with ourselves to push our limits and beliefs.
3. **Replace the word "but" from your vocabulary with "can."** When you wake up in the morning, be happy and grateful because you're alive and can accomplish anything you choose.
4. **The only person we have to prove anything to** is the person's image we see in the mirror.

That person in the mirror is the one holding you back from your destiny.

CHAPTER TWO

# Fuel up

Just like we fuel our vehicle for our trip, as a baby we had prepared for our destination in our life. The people in our lives made all kinds of weird, googly noises trying to make us give them even the slightest smile or facial expression. Maybe if they were fortunate, they'd get a giggle. They'd tell us what a good baby we were and how cute. When we got older, they'd reach their arms out to encourage us to take a few steps toward them, clapping with excitement.

We were very unbalanced at first, moving our bodies slightly to the left or right, but we focused on the person in front of us telling us to trust them, that they'd be there to catch us if we start to fall. We learned to trust because they encouraged us and built self-confidence in us. Once we had the confidence, we would venture on our own, standing by ourselves, letting go of our safety net of the furniture. We'd take a few steps, fall to the floor, crawl over to the furniture again, stand up and try it over and over again. We determined to walk no matter how many times we failed and lost our balance. Nothing was going to get in our way of keeping up with our older siblings, or just having the freedom to go everywhere and get into those cupboards that were mysteries. We were sure there was something to play with in them. We wanted to see the world from above, not crawling on the floor with rug burns on our knees.

Years go by and now we have graduated to a bike. We get on that bike, our helmets on tight, hands on the handlebars squeezing for dear life as our fear starts and we envision ourselves falling to the ground and getting hurt. With our training wheels on the bike, we're still a little wobbly, but then we remember the training wheels are still there to protect us and keep us safe, building our self-confidence. We zoom around the driveway feeling pretty proud of ourselves. Then the day arrives when someone brings out the dreaded wrench and removes our safety net of the training wheels. Now we're scared and that sense of fear sets in our minds again. Now we're old enough to remember when we've fallen and the pain of scraping our skin. It seems even more painful when we actually see the blood or scraped skin. Here we go focusing on our balance and trying to keep the bike straight and stay on the road. Every time we start to lose our balance, we feel the bike come upright again. We were building confidence and hearing that person behind us holding onto the back of our bike saying, "keep your balance," and "you can do it," encouraging us. Yahoo, we did it! We can now ride a bike by ourselves. Looking back can you remember how great you felt?

Years pass and now we're all grown up. We can walk, ride a bike and now we're learning to drive a vehicle. We study hard to pass the knowledge test, but now we're not getting the encouragement we received as a small child. Our parents might say, "you can pass," but now they throw the words at us "You just have to study," and "You have to pass this on your own. I can't be there this time."

They taught us to drive by example. If they are aggressive drivers with no respect for safety and the law, then we learned that unless someone now teaches us differently and we change those habits. You when it was coming to a stop or accelerating. You could tell by the gestures, by hearing the horn honking or the words that came out of their mouth. Some of those words you were told not to repeat.

Finally, it's your turn to get behind the wheel. Your parents instruct where the brake and gas pedal are. We learn to drive up and down the road, weaving from side to side, trying to keep the vehicle on our side of the road. Now, just like in the past, we have someone to encourage us and keep us focused in the direction we want to go to reach our goal. They're there to grab the wheel if we start to wander off in either direction. They're trying hard not to show their fear. We might get the occasional lecture because we lost our focus and scared them or ourselves.

Our parents ask us over and over, "why did you do that?" or "why didn't you pay attention?" We tell them we don't know because we really are unaware of why we did those things. We haven't learned what a paradigm is, how it controls our thinking and that our thoughts control our actions and results. We learn it's okay to make mistakes repeatedly because we're learning lessons and replacing bad habits of with good ones; we're becoming a safer, more responsible driver. We form the habit slowing down for a red light or looking around before we turn. We were taught as a child to be safe, it's like crossing a street we look both directions first. Playing it safe is really important, but when we get older, we allow fear to hold us back from becoming who we want to be or where we want to go.

When I had my driving school, I taught my students not to keep looking in the rearview mirror because even though it's important to keep checking what's behind you, it's more important to keep your eyes on the BIG picture in front of you. Keep your eyes and focus on where you want to go and what's around you. I wish I knew while teaching those students that thoughts create our results. That would've helped them realize why they're getting the results they're getting and how to overcome them by changing their thoughts.

The day has come for our road test and we're nervous. Fear, anxiety and doubt has taken over our mind. We've spent so many hours driving around and around learning the do's and don'ts of driving. We wait for the examiner to meet us. Our palms are sweaty and our brain is racing. We start driving and allow those good habits that we were taught to take over our thoughts and actions. Yahoo, we were successful and now we look at that license in our hands and visualize driving down the road. Freedom at last.

We can see ourselves behind the wheel, hear the music playing, singing to the tunes, hands on the steering wheel, waving at our friends as we drive by. Then our parents remind us that now we have to learn how to actually drive that vehicle safely. Our self-confidence rises and we feel like we can achieve anything. If unfortunately, you are unsuccessful, you don't give up, you just keep practicing and keep trying until you are successful.

Imagine when you went for your driving test, what were the feelings you had?

How did you feel the first time you drove alone?

CHAPTER THREE

# Intersection Ahead

Our adventure is on its way. We program our GPS with our destination coordinates. We're driving down the road feeling the warmth of the sun as it shines through the front windshield. The windows are down and we can feel the warm breeze on our bodies. We get excited and nervous talking about trip. We come across our first road sign, it's an intersection ahead sign. Once we arrive at the intersection, we turn off the radio, check the frequency of our GPS and it shows that we can choose any of the roads and we'll still reach where we want to be. We don't have a plan laid out, so we just pick one. We tune the radio to the frequency of the station we want to hear, the type of music we desire.

In our lifetime we come across so many intersection signs where we're not really sure which road to take. Sometimes our life's GPS won't tell us the right road to take. The thought of the unknown becomes scary to us. This is when our paradigms show up because we've brought our baggage full of our paradigms with us on our trip.

There are two parts to our minds that explain the things we think and the actions we take gives us the results we get.

**One part of the mind is the conscious mind** – The conscious mind is connected through our senses. We can hear, see, taste, smell and touch. Our senses gather information that has trained and conditioned us since birth and throughout our lives.

**One part of the mind is the sub-conscious mind** – The subconscious mind expresses emotions and feelings and whatever is impressed upon it. This expression is what we refer to as being in control of the **doing**. Paradigms can be positive or negative. They can hold you back, but actually it's you allowing the paradigms to control you and keep you in the stage you're at. You can recognize this and push yourself to let go and let go. **Release your inner child's imagination and have faith. Just like Peter Pan, we have to believe**.

A paradigm is a multitude of habits. A habit is an idea that's fixed in a person's subconscious mind that causes them to do something without any conscious thought. Thoughts create feelings.

A paradigm causes our behavior.

Throughout our lives, we do things we don't want to do. We don't realize our paradigms in the subconscious mind control our actions or behaviors. For a person to experience permanent change in their professional and personal life, there must be a change in the primary cause of their results. A common mistake is trying to change the results by changing the behavior. When this happens, the change is temporary. Behavior is a secondary cause. The primary cause is the paradigm. Our parents or whoever raised you most likely gave you your paradigms, but you are responsible for changing them.

Knowing and understanding the paradigm our first step because results come from behavior and behavior comes from our paradigms. The results explain how we are programmed. We're programmed from birth by our surroundings.

**Story Time**

One Sunday morning in church with my parents, I was bored and tired. My brother and some of my cousins decided we were going downstairs to the washrooms to play. We told our parents we had to go to the bathroom and went down the stairs feeling freedom at last. We ran around playing, not really noticing our voices were getting louder and louder. Then we heard the footsteps coming down the stairs. They weren't quiet steps, they weren't happy sounds.

We stopped as our dad stepped around the corner. The expression on his face matched his steps; it was not a happy face. We were in trouble, we were caught. I'm sure you can imagine how the rest of the story went.

The question is **why** did we yell in the basement when we knew better? We knew what the consequences were going to be. The answer is our paradigms. We knew the results, but we did it anyway because we didn't understand that our habits, our actions create our results. It wasn't something we had never done before, we knew if we were yelling and screaming when we were supposed to be quiet what would happen. The first time we ever did it, we were told not to do it again. The second time we were shown the results, but we kept doing it.

As I grew older, I'd sit in the pew and listen to my papa preach sermons and I really enjoyed it. The stories he told were so interesting. What I was hearing in my conscious mind made me feel happy and peaceful, so my subconscious mind accepted the fact that going to church and listening to sermons was good. When we're driving that vehicle over the speed limit, we know better. We know the results if we're caught on the policeman's radar, but we do it anyway.

## PARADIGM EXAMPLE

Do you remember eating supper as a child, and your plate had food on it like the dreaded asparagus or turnips? Those were some foods I didn't like. If your parents didn't like those foods do you think they would've cooked them for you? Probably not. I never cooked food for my daughters that I didn't like , so I never cooked turnips or asparagus and that was a paradigm of mine back then. If I didn't cook them, how did I know if my girls would like them or dislike them?

Imagine some things you did as a child that had bad results? What were they? Did you wish you made a different choice?

If you can remember some foods you tried imagine how they tasted. Were the foods sour, sweet, bitter?

CHAPTER FOUR

# Detour Ahead

We sometimes come across a detour sign on our trip that makes us worried. We feel self-doubt and fear of the unknown. We're starting to unpack some of those items in luggage #1 because it's a road we've never taken before.

Our paradigms start to stand out. The paradigm has an enormous influence over a person's conscious faculties. If and when you use your imagination, you generally unconsciously use it in a negative manner against yourself. An individual creates an image in their mind where they see the circumstance as the dominate role and sabotage their exciting journey. It's like us staring at the detour sign, allowing those doubts and fears, the negative imagination we envision to take our positive thoughts and excitement away from us. We start the "What if" game in our heads, assuming the negative and not the positive. Everything we want is on the other side of fear. We're not understanding the vibration in our body is not the right one. We're allowing our thoughts to control our results. We're opening the wrong luggage.

## OUR GPS HAS LOST ITS FREQUENCY

When our GPS loses frequency, does that mean we're lost forever, or has life just put us on a different road and we'll still find our way to our destination? We call it a side trip.

**Story Time**

I grew up in a house with four brothers. I was the only girl. Our dad was a truck driver, our mother owned restaurants. My parents were very sociable people, involved in the church and raising us kids. We had a cabin at Okanagan Lake in our early years. Some of my greatest memories as a child were at the lake. I remember Dad and my uncle Bobby building a dock with a high diving board, a low diving board and a slide. I used to climb the ladder to the top board just to lay on the board and explore what was under the water swimming by. I wouldn't jump because I had fear of what was further under the surface.

We're all like that little girl if we think about it. As long as we can see what's there we can decide if it's safe. Our conscious mind tells our subconscious mind. My mind was telling me that it's a long way from that high diving board to the water.

My dad would come to the cabin after work and he'd catch me lying on the high board. He'd be upset and say, "If you can show me you can jump off there safely, then you can be up there, if not come down." I'd climb back down the ladder.

One day I was day dreaming when I heard the same steps coming down the dock. By the time I stood up it was too late, dad was at the top of the ladder.

He said, "well?"

I knew what that meant. I had to jump to show him that if I fell off, I was safe.

He knew I could swim, but I had to face my fear at that moment and jump. He started walking closer to me and before he could get too close, I took the plunge and ran and jumped, plugging my nose on the way down. I hit the water and started moving my body to get me back up the surface. It was literally sink or swim. I swam to the shore where my dad was waiting for me and I was so excited that I did. I never realized that I'd faced a terror barrier in my life. Sometimes in life we need someone to push us to make that jump. Maybe they know our potential better than we do, or maybe it's just to help us get over our fear of the unknown.

## TERROR BARRIERS

Ideas are a collection of thoughts coming together. Thoughts are a form of energy. Because the energy that flows through us can be negative or positive, that flow determines the vibration we put ourselves in. A person's vibration is the way we're feeling. The feeling could be bad or good.

When we're changing direction on the road to our destination, we'll feel all sorts of different vibrations. It's how we understand and handle the situation that gives us our results. When we come across a detour in our lives, we can try a different road without exploring the road we're on and play it safe. Or we can go for it and face the terror barrier head on by making that jump. We can unpack some of our baggage of anxiety, doubt, worry and fear, or let go and let God and believe in ourselves. We can be excited and ready for the growth that comes with breaking through that terror barrier.

Sometimes we're not the only barrier. There could be other people, insecure about these **paradigms telling us that we can't do it**. It reminds me of playing Red Rover as a child. Do you know the game? There are two teams of people holding hands tightly standing in a line. The object is to break through the other team's line.

They chant "Red Rover, Red Rover, Send ...... Right over." We are praying they won't call our name because we see the strength of the people in that line and we start convincing ourselves that we are too weak and will never break through their line.

Our name gets called and we feel the energy in our body changing and our vibration changes into "go for it, I can do it." We look for the weakest section that to break through. We make eye contact and pretend that we are going to break through one section, then we start to run. It's at that moment we break through that terror barrier, we have made that jump. We either break through their chain or have to join their team and learn how we can do it better and succeed next time.

Even if we don't break through, we should be proud of ourselves for trying. If we look back throughout our lives, we can remember so many situations where we had to face those barriers and think about our choice and the results. We can't become who we want to be if we remain where we are. If we keep saying that we want different results, then we need to change some habits and direction in our lives. If we stay in the same frequency, we'll always listen to the same music. We need to get that thought from the conscious mind to the subconscious mind to put that idea into action to get the results we desire. Get into the vibration of that frequency you want. Playing it safe always gives the same results.

It may not seem obvious, but attaining the goal itself isn't important. What's important is who you become along the way.

The beginning of is scary.

The middle of life is exciting.

The end of life is sad.

The end of life doesn't have to be sad if you've done the things you wanted, if you broke those barriers and made that jump many times. The end of life is sad if you've allowed your paradigms or other people to influence you and hold you back.

Don't get to the end of your life and say "I wish that I would have." Our mistake is we think we need to know how to achieve those goals and have every step laid out so we believe it'll happen. We need to see it in our imaginations before. Our job is to set a goal, write it down, envision it and pretend it's already happening, just like when we were children. It was so easy back then to be that pretend person. We dressed, talked and acted just like that person we idolized, so why did we stop? We can accomplish anything if we believe in our dreams and ourselves. We need to lose that programming that has been instilled in our minds since we were babies. We need to stop thinking that once we achieve our goal it ends there. This the exciting part; this is where it begins again. New adventures, new dreams, new lessons, new vibrations. New people come into our lives. The roads are endless and so is your life. Try new things, go to new places, become so many different people. You don't have to be the person sitting in the back of the room, be the person up front teaching the class.

Imagine if Thomas Edison, the Wright brothers, Oprah or so many others gave up, where would we be? Where would they be? We are who we are, not the person everyone else thinks we should be.

We are special, unique people with gifts and passions that need to burst out of our inner self. We'll reach our goals, but it's the lessons and the people who we've touched along the way that's the greatest gift.

When we reach our goals, others feel the positive vibration and the positive energy your body is radiating. You'll attract more of that same energy from others. That's why it's so important to be around like-minded people. Be around people who encourage you, accept you as you are and celebrate your achievements. People who say you can't achieve your goals are usually the ones with the fear. They don't understand that you're different; that you're willing to do what it takes to achieve your goals. It's their paradigm that's the issue.

My dad used tell my brothers and me, "You don't have to be like everyone else and do what everyone else does. If your friends jumped off the bridge it doesn't mean you have to." Little did my dad realize that I already did jump off a bridge in Ashton Creek because my friends did. I figured if I could jump off the high diving board and be okay, if I jumped off the bridge, my results would be the same. And they were.

Throughout my life I've tried and accomplished so many things. There were other things I wanted to do, but I allowed my fears and paradigms take control. Some people say to me "why don't you just settle for one thing and be happy?"

Other people call me a gypsy and tell me they wish they could be brave enough to try different things. It has nothing to do with bravery, it's simply setting my mind to it and allowing my subconscious mind to put my ideas into action. I wasn't aware why I did things, or that this process was going on, but now I am. That's why I'm sharing it with you.

I had a teacher ask all the students to write out what goals they'd like to achieve after they graduate. My goal was to be a teacher. I remember when he read mine he looked at me and laughed, "Why do you think you can become a teacher? You're not smart enough or have good enough grades. Just get married and have babies."

I graduated from high school was married the following year. I delivered my first daughter the year after that my second daughter the following year. I didn't know it, but I was living the same life as my mother because that's what I believed girls did when they finished school. I was living her blue print. I heard my teacher telling me these things and I believed him and so many others.

When my girls started growing up, I decided there was so much life out there to be explored and I wanted to try some different things. I loved being a mom and wife, and I had support from my husband. We moved outside of Williams Lake and that's where my life started to change. Chimney Lake had an association and it was election time. I was nominated as a vice president and I thought "how hard can that be?" I was elected and my life was about to change. A few years passed and I was elected president. I hit a terror barrier when I had to conduct my first meeting. I was terrified. Why would I do this to myself? I don't know how to conduct a meeting or write newsletters, and I certainly don't know how to present myself with government officials discussing plans for the community like paving the roads and private telephone lines. I quickly bought a book to help me. I read the book and held my first meeting. My meetings went off without any problems. I broke through that barrier and learned that I really enjoyed public speaking. I didn't realize it, but I was changing my frequency and that was changing my vibration, which changed my thoughts about myself and my results.

I decided to do some sermons at our church. I discovered that I enjoyed that too. This was a new road for me.

We never know where the roads we travel will lead us and what adventures we'll have along the way. My life was zig zagging and taking many detours in the next few years. I had to break through many barriers and replace many old paradigms that were holding me back and replace them with new ones.

Our children were grown and moved away from home. I had very bad empty nest as people call it. It was another new road for me to drive down, not knowing what to do with my life. I didn't think I had a purpose; my job was done. I felt like I was taking a detour and my vehicle's GPS lost its signal. I wanted someone to tell me what to do. I wanted to dial in that frequency to get that vibration I had years earlier when I was with the flow of energy. I remember if the phone rang, I'd look at it. If it wasn't one of my girls I wouldn't answer because it wasn't the frequency I asked for. I was so mad because I wasn't getting help from anyone to tell me what to do.

I was on a poor me pity party, stuck in the road and wanting someone to pull me out and tell me what lies ahead. I needed to wake up and realize that, yes that part of my life was gone but a new one is waiting to be explored. I needed to look back at all the positive things in my life and be proud of who I have become. I survived years of raising children and we were all still friends.

Our oldest daughter got married, moved eight hours away and gave birth to our first grandchild, a precious little girl. We traveled to see her as much as possible, but she was growing up so fast. One day I told my husband I'd lost my purpose and we needed to move closer to our grandchildren since now our second grandchild was on its way.

He looked as if I'd lost my marbles. My husband drove truck part time and supervised at a local plywood plant. I asked him which job he enjoyed most. He told me it was driving truck.

I asked him what his passion is.

He told me, "My passion is driving. It gives me energy, it's a new adventure every day, and I'm good at it, why?"

I said "I was thinking." Those words always scared him because I was either going to give him a project or I was about to take us on a new adventure, down a new road. I'm so grateful to have such an understanding husband because he believed in me. He said I have such a powerful gift of teaching and helping people that he wouldn't stand in my way and he'd be there whatever I wanted to do. I remember telling him that the road I was on isn't the one I want to be on. I want to be a teacher.

My husband sat me down and asked me to focus on his words and believe in them. He said, "When you were the president of the association at the lake you were teaching, when you were preaching sermons to the congregation you were teaching and when you home-schooled the girls you were teaching."

I never realized I was achieving my goal from high school. The one the teacher said I'd never do because I wasn't smart enough and didn't have the personality for it. Maybe I didn't have a college degree to teach, but I was teaching in a different way. I realized that not everyone had to have a college education to be successful at their dreams or goals.

My husband and I broke the terror barrier and believed in ourselves. We stopped listening to others telling us that we were making a mistake. They said my husband had been at the mill for 30 years, why give up that security. I thought, what security? The company can close their doors at any time. It's the security you have in yourself that's important.

If you don't have a secure feeling about yourself inside, then you need to change your self-image. We moved up north not even having a place to live or jobs to go to. All we had was a want to be near our grandkids and the desire to make it happen. We made a decision and put it into action. We moved and a new life began. My husband got a driving job right away, and I had a job offer to become a driver examiner. We were both scared about our new road, but we had a feeling we were on the way to our destination. I had to go to Vancouver for training and my paradigms showed up. I started to have doubts and fears. I was unpacking that luggage from my trunk that I didn't want in my life. From the time that I got the job until I went for training my thoughts were going crazy. I knew that I could do it, and I had my family's support, but then people tried to put doubts in my mind. I knew it was because they don't understand.

Detours can be positive and great lessons with no curves in the road even when we lose our GPS. Have you ever had so many curves and times that you were stuck or had a flat tire on a detour and thought it was a sign that you'd made a mistake? Maybe you should've listened to those people and their doubts? Did you keep going? Did you journal all your adventures? Did you feel so blessed for what you saw and the growth you had along the way? I bet you did. I bet you said, "Thank you, thank you, thank you." We're not the same person after taking detours. If we take the good and throw away the bad, we'll be one step closer to becoming who we want to be.

Can you imagine how your life might have turned out differently?

Can you imagine how freeing you from those fears has made you who you are today?

Can you remember some choices you made on your own without listening to other people saying you couldn't do what you wanted?

CHAPTER FIVE

# STOP

We've been successful without our GPS losing its frequency and have had an adventure but are now driving back on course to our destination. Sometimes losing our life's GPS gives us the best life lessons and allows us meet the most amazing people.

We come to a stop sign. We look around to make sure it's safe and then continue on our journey. Our lives sometimes are like stop signs. Situations appear and we reassess our path. We may not have come to a detour, but we stop and wonder if we should continue because the road 'we've just been down has worn us out. It's mentally drained us and we want to give up on our journey. We sometimes think we've lost the ability to imagine what it will feel like at the end of our trip. When we're growing up we sometimes forget to use our imagination and it's so sad because when we stop imagining we're losing our frequency and that great vibration. We need to get back into that frequency of positive energy and stop aligning with negative energy. We need to close our eyes and imagine how it will be at our destination.

**Story Time**

I was a driver examiner for a few years and I loved the people I've met. I'm grateful for all the life lessons and experiences. I made such great friendships. My life had come to a stop sign. I stopped and when I looked around, I once again had lost the vibration I was seeking. I was on a different frequency. I realized that I hadn't been living my passion with teaching. I wanted to help teach these drivers to become safer and why the examiners mark the way they do. I wanted to show them the safety behind the scores on their tests to help them become safe drivers. I knew I'd make the roads safer by doing this.

I decided to go for more training, but this time to become a driving instructor. My youngest daughter, Marilyn and I left for Vancouver for training. Marilyn decided she wanted to take this course also. Who was I to discourage her after all the different roads I've been down? I didn't know where this would take her, so I encouraged her and we signed up for the course. I felt pretty confident about the course because I had been an examiner. I felt I could help Marilyn when she came upon her terror barriers. My husband came with us and we stayed at our aunt's house. Marilyn's son was taken care of by my husband and his aunt. We were so grateful to have such support and encouragement. We made it through the course and we both learned so much about the course and ourselves. We broke through many barriers and replaced so many negative paradigms with positive ones. We were on the same frequency, so we fed off of each other's vibration to be successful and pass the course.

We arrived home and started training students right away. I look back and see I had to deal with so many people's habits while teaching them to drive. I had to teach the students new habits and replace the old ones they developed from other people. There were so many different personalities, it was so interesting to get to know the students and their families.

Now that I understand the mind, I have to look back and laugh. So many times I'd put on my brake as we were going to run a stop sign. They'd ask me why and I'd tell them, "because there's a stop sign and stop means stop.

Some students said their parents told them to make sure no one's coming. Others had the misconception they didn't have to wait for pedestrians because the pedestrian was a hazard as they were walking on the cross walk.

I remember asking so many times: "Why didn't you stop before you turned right at a red light? Why didn't you look behind you as you backed up? Why didn't you look in the other lane before you moved over? This is after many times of explaining what to do and why we do it. The answer was always "I don't know."

I know now why it happened, and I find it so interesting that we do things over and over again and it's only through repetition that we can change. It would be rewarding and I was so proud when my students passed their driving tests. I can see now how sometimes the students aren't successful because they let their fear take over and their results are not what they had hoped. Sometimes they'd get upset at me or their parents blamed me. I never got upset because I'd read their tests and explain that I never taught them to run a stop sign or speed through a school zone. I just explained that they were nervous and could take it again. I knew the reasons everyone thought what they did.

Can you imagine when you first started driving how many times you made the same mistakes over and over, but through repetition and determination you became successful.

Can you remember not applying for a job because you never had the confidence or listened to that little voice in your head saying you're not good enough?

Imagine how if you would have just gone for that interview or taken that course, how it would have changed your destination. Remember your destination is not just a one time thing, every time you reach it, you've grown and now you want more.

**Wow! Stop! Red Light! Detour!** Sometimes in our lives, things happen to us that we believe are bad and we think we've definitely taken the wrong road. We think our life has come a stop or we're on the wrong road and can't get off.

**Story Time**

Years passed I was still teaching. My daughter had taken time off to have another baby, so now we will have been blessed with six grandchildren. Two boys and four girls. We were happy with our jobs and were so grateful that both our girls and their families lived close by. One day I received a call from Marilyn saying that she had numbness on the right side of her body.

Marilyn had a very strict workout routine and lived a very healthy life. I assumed it was a pulled muscle but told her to go get it checked. She called me later and said the doctor thought it was a pulled muscle also. The next day she called again, but this time I could tell by her voice that she was really worried.

The numbness had spread to her head and leg. She went to the hospital and they were concerned so they made her an appointment to see a doctor in Grand Prairie. She was scheduled to be there the next morning when she got a call telling her to go straight to Edmonton University Hospital. Her husband packed up the kids and decided to make a little trip of it. She thought she'd only have tests done and return home. The doctors kept her overnight for more tests. The next day I received a call from Marilyn that I'll never forget. She said, "Mom I've just seen the doctor and my tests came back. I have MS."

I was in shock and didn't know what to say. My first words were "how did you get this?"( Stop the car and let's go back in time). I really didn't know much about MS because it never affected my family. I knew other people with the disease, but when it's not part of your life a person might not understand much about it. Marilyn went for more tests again and again. We learned more about the disease and how it affects everybody differently. I also never mentioned that Marilyn has one daughter with spinal bifida and her son was born with a club foot.

Anyone who knows Marilyn knows she's a strong-willed woman and doesn't sit around pitying herself. We just dealt with things as they happened. We took our grandson to Vancouver Children's Hospital every month for the first year of his life for a new cast as he grew. Once he turned one the doctors gave him Botox injections in his ankle. Dion is now 11 years old and has no issues with his foot. Our granddaughter who the doctor said would never walk, runs, plays and wrestles with her siblings.

When Marilyn was diagnosed with the disease, she was determined it wouldn't' control their lives and it wouldn't win. She lives everyday as a blessing and a gift from God. She now uses her disease as a platform to help others. She has blogs and has helped encourage and support other families with MS. She has such a positive outlook on life. When she relapses she just uses her positive thinking to get the results she wants with what she's living with. We are so grateful and blessed to have two strong daughters who never give up and believe in themselves. They are strong role models for their children and us as their parents.

If you're stuck, use the energy from within your body and change the frequency. Change where you dial for help like you'd dial a tow truck if you're stuck in the road. Use the directories for the contacts to help get you to where you want to go. If you have or are having a difficult time in your life, be sure to use that as a time to make you stronger, to grow along the way to your goal.

Your legacy is not what you leave behind, but the people you've touched in the world. How you were someone's lighthouse to guide them.

We never know what will happen on the roads we take. We may wonder why something happened, but we have to remember every person we meet, every event that has occurred, happened to make us who we're supposed to be. Sometimes we attract events like what happened to Marilyn. Other people needed to hear her story and still have to hear her story, so they can overcome and change their own frequency and vibration. They now share Marilyn's frequency by sharing their situations, and in turn, will help others change their lives. If your boat becomes just broken pieces floating in the water, use those broken pieces to hang onto to swim to shore. People think they need the whole boat to get them to their goal, but it's not always like that. It's the pieces or life preservers along the way that help you get through the tough times .

Our eldest daughter Nichole has overcome so many paradigms in her life. While she was public school the teacher called me said she needed to see a doctor because she was having a hard time in school and couldn't concentrate. I was so upset they said that in front of her. She cried and didn't want to go back to school where she felt everyone thought she was stupid and would make fun of her. I decided to home school her to help her learn different ways to remember things.

We sang songs relating to her assignments. I realized that she was a hands-on person and very social. What a great quality to have. Nichole graduated and became a parts manager in a vehicle dealership. She is doing something she loves, she constantly meets new people and loves learning about the vehicles. Nichole went for training and was so successful her self-image sky-rocketed. These are examples how the words people say and their judgement can affect your life and your goals if you allow them to. When you learn to understand that you are not those words, you realize that you are you and can do anything if you really want it. My daughters are so different in so many ways, but I've told them time and time again, "Be who you want to be not, who dad or I, or anyone else thinks you should be. Design your own blueprint."

Don't live my dreams, create your own. I am so proud of my daughters in everything they do in their lives because they are themselves and unique women. Have you sat back as a parent and gave your child the encouragement to go down their own road, or do you still want to control them? If you are still trying to control them are you trying to protect them? How are they going to learn from their failures and become stronger people if you don't allow them to make their own mistakes to learn?

I decided a few years ago to put teaching driving lessons on hold and become an air brake instructor. I was raised around trucks my whole life. My dad took me driving plenty of times growing up. Maybe it was just so he could sing to me like he loved to do, but I had a lot to learn. I spent many hours in trucks to gain more knowledge. I had a very good friend who was a driver instructor who taught commercial driving. He taught me so much and was kind enough to have me help him with repairs or maintenance on his trucks so I could learn more. I sat in on a couple of his air brakes courses to get experience. I went to Vancouver and passed my instructors license.

Remember, this was a huge fear that I had to conquer . I had to change my paradigm of fear and replace it with the attitude that I could do anything. My goal is always there in front of me, I just have to believe to achieve. I had to imagine and envision myself already teaching the classes and being very successful. I was a high achiever so I wouldn't allow myself to quit or be unsuccessful. Maybe it was to prove to myself that I wasn't the person that other people told me I was or couldn't become.

I taught air brake classes for a couple of years, then I some people told me I should become certified so I could teach and test the students as there was only one other place in the city offering that service. I was so confident and proud of myself that I said yes. Once the arrangements were made everything was falling into place especially my paradigms. I was letting my fear and doubt take over. I was losing my frequency and losing that vivid picture in my mind of me succeeding, of being certified. What happens if I fail? What will others think? I'll feel so defeated and stupid. Will they think it was wasted time? Man, those negative thoughts were taking over my whole body and I was allowing them to. I did a lot of praying and spent the next few days alone trying to tell myself a different story. I believed I felt pressured because I was more worried about what others would think, what the men would think having a woman teach them about the air brake system on a truck. I was focused on the negative so I had to start replacing my negative thoughts with positive ones. I had to tell myself "girl, you are good at teaching this. You're a woman and because of that you have a different teaching technique. You're a story teller and love to make people laugh and have fun." I knew when people have fun they'd learn quicker and understand it. I wanted to make sure when they left my class they had self-worth and a positive attitude with positive energy surrounding them. In the end, it went very well and I achieved what I set out to do. I was successful at becoming a certified assessment officer.

Do you remember the movie *The Wizard of Oz*? All Dorothy wanted was to go home, the Tin Man wanted a heart, the Lion courage and the Scarecrow a brain. After many roads travelled, they discovered everything they were looking for was right in front of them the whole time. All each of them had to do was envision it and believe they already had it. That is such a great lesson for my air brakes students. Every person we meet, even if it's for a short time or a lifetime, has been put in our lives for a purpose for them and us. I am in my student's lives teaching them this course because some need to learn a different way and have encouragement. It was the yellow brick road that was the journey and answer they were looking for. They were placed in order because they had the same frequency to get something at the end of the road, their destination or goal. Are you on your yellow brick road? Who has crossed your path to help you get where you want to go?

My journey down the road of a certified air brake instructor has taught me so many things. It has opened up so many new roads, so many new chapters in my life and others. I've overcome the paradigm that teaching air brakes was just for me. I've had so many men come into my class and look around waiting to see the instructor. When I introduce myself, some are surprised and say out loud, "but you're a woman."

My response is, You bet. The last time I looked in the mirror I was." Some people don't even think about it. It's been a wild ride. Two years ago I taught a woman who's a great friend of mine. She asked me what I liked about teaching the class. I told her teaching the people, helping them, making the course fun and having them walk away from my class with self-worth.

I talked to the woman about the course and I was sold. Now a few years before that I had a friend who was interested in purchasing one of my trucks but at that time I was not interested. I needed it to examine my students on their air test. While I was talking to this woman on the phone, I asked her how much for the course. She told me the price and when I hung up I was excited and scared but knew that this is the new road that I wanted to go down. I knew that I wanted to take that detour and it would take me closer to my destination. I called my friend and asked if he was still interested in my truck and he replied yes and I said how much do you want to pay and he said the exact amount that I needed for the course and it was what I was hoping to get from it. I knew that it was meant to be so I sold the truck and paid for the course.

I hit so many paradigms and did a lot of soul-searching and self-evaluation. My life has been changed and it was the people that were put in place in my life that helped me make it possible. My success was there the whole time, but I had to have everything in order to accept it. After I completed the Thinking into Results program, I decided that I was ready to become a certified consultant. I made it happen and had my coach, my friend who helped me. No matter who understands or accepts my journey on this new road it's okay. They have their own paradigms to overcome. I accept my new life and my journey. I'm responsible for my own actions and accomplishments. I've opened up my life to attract diverse opportunities and the more I attract, the more positive energy I release back out to the universe.

Can you relate to something happens in your life that stops you in your tracks?

CHAPTER SIX

# No U Turn Permitted

There comes a time when we've gone so far that we tell ourselves, "There's no turning back now." That's a positive thing. It means we've broken through so many obstacles that have been put in front of us by using our higher mental faculties such as:

**Memory:** Some of us have weak ones, some of us have strong ones.

**Reason:** It allows us to think, and those thoughts become ideas. This is why it's so important to have positive ideas. Our feelings come from our ideas. Our feelings turn into our actions and create our results .

**Perception:** Our opinion or point of view; the way we see things. Just because we don't agree with someone doesn't mean either one is wrong or right, it just means that we see things differently. If our perception is different, we must learn to respond not react.

**Imagination:** Using our vision to pretend or fantasize like did when we were children. It allows us to create a picture in our mind. If you can play along with me and go to that beach with me, you'll realize how easy it will be to keep that goal so close to becoming your life. Let's close our eyes and relax, let's imagine that we're at a beach. If we have a strong imagination, we actually feel the warm breeze, feel the sand under our feet, the heat from the sun. We can hear the waves as they splash on the shore. This is why imagination is such an important part of reaching your goals.

**Will:** Part of the imagination. You must have the will and concentration to keep that picture or vision in your mind. You must want it and believe it so much that you already live it. If you start losing that feeling and vibration, tune back into that frequency. Close your eyes and use your imagination again.

**Intuitive Factor:** It can pick up on your body's vibrations. When something happens, you have a vibration that gives you a feeling. It's either good or bad, so you're picking up a positive or negative intuitive factor or feeling.

Imagine situations using each of the factors.

**Story time**

My husband and I decided to move from the north of B.C. and live where I was born and raised. I moved first to get things in order. Some people told us we were crazy to live apart for that long, but we looked at the big picture and knew everything had to be in order to fall into place where it should be. The order was that we had to both learn to grow up a lot and learn to grow into who we were meant to be. The path since I moved here wasn't what I ever thought was waiting for me. I remember my husband calling me excited because he cooked his first full meal by himself. I remember calling him telling him the fear I had flying to Toronto for the training. I had never flown alone. We have broken so many terror barriers and grown up so much. My daughters would say, "one day you two will make great adults." They teased me and told me I'm a big girl now.

When I became a certified consultant with a program, I was very confident. Many times I had strong heart to heart chats with myself. I told myself, "remember you're in the driver's seat now. There's no one holding their hands over yours to help you. You have been given all the tools you need to get you to where you want to go. You are the one turning the steering wheel to steer you in the direction you want to drive. If you choose to stray and speed, then you must be prepared to receive the ticket, learn that lesson and move on. Telling the police officer you didn't know why you did it won't work."

We have all the books and help out there in the universe, we just have to decide if we're going to accept it and keep driving, or reject it, make that illegal u turn and head back. I told myself that I was driving on. Once I made that decision, doors opened and ideas came flooding from within me.

We never had Christmas growing up in our house. We respected our parent's decision, but boy I loved those twinkling lights on the Christmas trees. My mom's parent's had Christmas. I can still close my eyes and see my grandma's homemade pies sitting on the counter. I can smell her delicious dinners. My birthday is close to Christmas, so I'd go over and decorate their tree every year. I can envision my grandpa getting out the ladder. I'd climb the steps until I was tall enough to put the top ornament on. He would hand me the tinsel strands one by one. I dreamed of one day having my own tree and decorations at my house.

It doesn't matter how many years ago that was because those memories are in my mind and all I have to do is close my eyes, use my senses and they are right there again. I would be wearing the dress that my grandma handmade for me and she'd take pictures. My first Christmas was spending Christmas eve at my uncle Bobby's and auntie Dianne's. I remember the black dress I received as a present under the tree. Visioning is so powerful because I can close my eyes and see that dress as though it's right in front of me. We moved to Williams Lake years later and I became with friends with a girl. Her family was so great to me I felt like they were my own. The family invited me to spend a Christmas Eve with them and we exchanged gifts. I was able to see how other people celebrated Christmas and I was so grateful.

This family that I became part of actually appeared in my life years before that move to Williams Lake. I was a little girl and my parents were both at work. There was a knock on the door so I opened it. There was a grandpa, grandma, dad, mom and their three children. The Grandpa proceeded to explain that they used to live in this house when their son, who was standing here next to me, was a little boy. He asked if they could please come in and look around.

"Well of course you can" I said.

After they were finished in the house, they wanted a picture of the kids in front. They asked if a couple of my brothers and I would stand with them, so we did. Now let's go ahead years later in Williams Lake. I arrived at my new school really scared, not knowing anyone. A girl came up and introduced herself. We became friends and I was invited for supper at her house to meet her family. We proceeded to talk about where I moved from. Her dad mentioned that he used to live in Enderby when he was a boy.

He said he lived in a big house on Regent Street. I told him that's where I lived. They all stopped talking and the mom went into her room for a while. When she came out, she asked if I remembered a family coming to walk through the house and taking pictures outside with some of their children.

I did because my parents weren't happy that I let strangers in the house. She put the picture on the table, and I looked. Here I am, one of the children in that picture many years before. People might be shocked at this true story, but now I understand that all those years ago we were in each other's life for a reason, actually many reasons. They were put in mine and I was put in theirs. It has been a few years now that my friends parents have passed, but I think of them all the time and they will always have a special place in my heart. I'm so very grateful for our imagination so I can go back and relive those wonderful times we shared and how much they were part of my life. I can still hear their voices and words of wisdom.

Let's go ahead some years after I finished school. I had just gotten married and my husband's family loved Christmas and did it all. We did the midnight mass celebration, came back to his parents' place to open gifts and have a snack . One Christmas the family decided to give their mom and dad a special gift of a written letter of special memories from each of us to share about being in the family. I hadn't been in the family long, so I decided to write a story called "looking through a child's eyes."

I want you to close your eyes and take the journey back in time with me to imagine how it was. Imagine experiencing the excitement of Christmas as a child. Feel how excited you were to see the tree lit for the first time. For me, it was a new experience having my own first Christmas. For the first time I had my own tree my tree in my own house. Decorating the house, I would sit in the dark at night and just stare at my ceiling watching the reflection of the lights as they twinkled. It was magic. I sang Christmas carols and danced in the living room remembering how I watched my grandparents dance in theirs. Can you smell your mom's baking in the kitchen? It smelt of sugar and spice in my house, for the first time.

I wrote in that letter that I understood what Christmas was like looking through a child's eyes. We are so blessed to go back and forth in our imagination to bring back fond memories. We only see what our brain is in harmony with, so let's get our brain in harmony with visioning and living the way we want to live. My first baby was born on Christmas day and now I have seven Christmas trees. It wasn't about the presents, just the feeling of joy and happiness – the peace I feel at that time of year. My daughters laugh and tell my mom that because I never had Christmas as a child, I was taking it out on them with all the trees and decorations, but they love it. It's the feeling, the vibration and the energy of the holidays that's so special.

Years passed and I was so excited I joined groups in Enderby to help others. I was asked to coordinate Santa's workshop. I loved Christmas, but had never heard of this. The group had done this for years and once I understood it, I jumped on board feet first not knowing what to do. I did know if it was an exciting and scary feeling and for a great cause, it was the right thing to do.

This volunteer group provides a store where people donate toys and items to be sold to children for gifts for their families. These items are so reasonable that the kids get really excited to be able to buy something for everyone in their family. The elves from the group wrap the gifts for the children. The proceeds go to the local schools for their meals program, to local food banks and to seniors for clothing and personal items. This event is so rewarding for everyone involved, the merchants who donate, the helpers, the people who donate items from their own homes. This is what it's all about. Putting yourself out there to help provide service to others is the most rewarding feeling. Leaving everyone you meet with a feeling of joy or purpose reflects that feeling back to you. Just smiling at a stranger or maybe giving a compliment can change their whole vibration. When our actions show we have a positive vibration of energy radiating from us, others feel it. I was Mrs. Christmas.

**Story Time: Manifesting**

Be careful what you manifest. When I was a little girl, my Uncle Bobby and Auntie Dianne had this little green Datsun. They would pick me up so I could babysit for them. I used to tell my aunt that when I grew up I wanted this car. I have no idea why, but something inside me just thought it was the coolest car. I should have been more specific because when I turned sixteen my dad said he had bought me a car. I was all excited expecting some sports car, but he said I had to go to Burns Lake to pick it up. I had never driven a standard transmission, and I must have forgotten that the green Datsun was a standard. My brother drove me there and Uncle Ernie let me practice on a back road to help me. When it was time to go to Prince George to where my dad was working, I did pretty well on the highway, but not so well at my first set of lights. I stalled the car and my legs were shaking so bad that I couldn't control the pedals. It didn't help when the guy in the truck behind me started honking his horn and I could see in my mirror that he wasn't a happy camper. My brother had to run down the road, push me over and drive my car through the intersection. I made it to the shop where my dad was. When he came out my brother kissed the ground and said, "I thought she was a goner."

I manifested that car by putting it out in the universe years before. It was in order and alignment that I received it, but I wished my driving was more aligned with the car.

My dad ended up driving it home as my brother explained he was scared for my life. I was scared to drive it to school, so I found a friend to drive it if I gave him free ride to school. I thought I was pretty smart until one day my dad was leaving the house at the same time I was and said he'd follow me.

Uh oh that wasn't good. I told my friend I had to drive alone. I pulled up to the first light and looked in my mirror. Dad was right behind me. All those fears from my first light experience came flashing back in my mind. My legs started shaking, my heart was racing. If I had just faced the fear and gone through the terror barrier the first time I would've been fine. The light turned green and I took my foot off the clutch and pushed on the throttle. I'm shocked that I never took out the clutch as the tires were spinning and smoking and I squealed through the intersection. I looked in my rearview and noticed my dad way behind me. I went on my merry way to school, waited until everyone left the parking lot then chugged home.

That night my dad asked me how many times I drove to school.

I said, "A few, why?"

He said he was curious.

I asked him, "How come it took you so long to catch up?"

"I was crawling back up onto the seat. I was hiding from the rocks and gravel your tires threw at me as you drove away," he told me. He decided he better take me out for some practice. With confidence, I broke through the fear for good this time. Manifesting does work! I learned when I manifest a vehicle I should be more specific.

Over the years I've manifested so many things into my life, both positive and negative. I worked at a hotel cleaning rooms and at the Christmas party, the grand door prize was an all-expenses paid trip to Hawaii. I went around for weeks telling my friends and family that I was going to win. At the end of the night my name was the last one in the barrel and I won.

Televised hockey games gave away prizes when the home team scored a goal. The winner's name was put on the screen for viewers to see. At the last game of the year and the last goal, my name was chosen and broadcasted. The funny thing is, two days prior my daughter was borrowing my vacuum cleaner and it broke. I told her I'd find a way to get a new one. My prize from the hockey game was a vacuum cleaner. I had people call me that I haven't heard from in twenty-five years to say they saw my name on TV.

One Valentine's Day, the local radio station had drawings all day long for dinners. I wanted to win a dinner for my husband so I kept calling, but no success. I finally got through and they announced I was the last caller of the day and won the grand prize. It was a trip to a ski resort for three days. I didn't know how to ski. I was terrified, but grateful. I told them that I didn't know how to ski, so they even threw in lessons.

We arrived at the resort and I was standing at the top of the hill staring down, my legs shaking. All I could hear was the coach encouraging me. I stood there until I heard a little boy yell up at me, "Hey lady, eventually you have to ski down the bunny hill because we're all waiting for you." I faced my fear and embarrassment and took the leap of faith. It was like jumping off that high diving board again. I survived and made it down the bunny hill with no broken bones. I was so proud of myself because I had conquered my fear and survived.

Some people say that I've been lucky, but there's a difference between luck and acquiring what you want. It's a desire and belief.

I decided to do a vision board and on it I described a store. I saw a "for rent" sign on the door. I was so excited; I quickly called the owner. I was too late; someone had just signed the papers. I was disappointed, but he had another space for rent there. I rushed to meet him and signed the papers. My vibration changed and I was ready to live my dream. I had a smile from ear to ear. I knew I could meet so many more people and give them the tools to change their lives just like I did. I'm proof that manifesting really works, but you have to really feel it, vision it, and believe that it will happen. It might not happen instantly, but don't give up. When it comes into alignment it will happen. Let's create our positive results.

Since then I have really grown. I started a Women in Business group to encouraging female business owners to support each other, to go for their goals, believe in themselves, boost their self-image and become who they want to be. I feel if I can teach air brakes to mostly men and break barriers to achieve my goals, I want to share my knowledge and experiences with others. I took a program by Peggy McCall on becoming an author, "The Committed Author," because I've always wanted to write a book. This course was amazing. Peggy's life experiences and knowledge made this next road to my destination so much easier. I was able to envision myself as a number one bestselling author already. I have created a workbook to go with my book as a self-help course to inspire people to change.

I can envision myself signing my books here in my office, signing people up to the "Thinking into Results" program and encouraging them to sign up for all the programs available. If they have always wanted to write a book, I am sharing my mentor with them. I can see myself going from city to city, sharing my story to full houses, meeting many people and helping them change their lives. I know sometimes that my number one baggage will come out of the trunk, but now it doesn't scare me because I know it's part of my growth and I can put them back in the trunk and lock them where they belong. I'm working on opening up my own Christmas store where I can sell my book and all the other courses that I provide. It has taken awhile to have things align that I put in place to manifest so many years ago, but it's happening and I'm open to receive it.

**Life as a caterpillar**

Have you ever studied caterpillars? To people who look at them, they are just a type of worm that crawls around hoping not to get stepped on. Those caterpillars have no idea that one day they will be in a cocoon all dark and secluded. They have no idea when they come out of that cocoon they've developed wings and are free to fly because they've transformed into a beautiful butterfly. We are like that caterpillar, we get to the point in our lives where we wonder what our purpose is. Why is nothing happening that we want to happen? We are evolving, but we just don't see it. Sometimes the answers we're looking for are right in front of us. Sometimes we give up too soon because we think something better or someone better is the road to follow, but if we stay on the road, the answer is right around the corner – We'll have wings to try new things, become who we want to become. We have evolved from being carried in someone's womb to someone's arms, we have crawled and learned how to run. We have learned how to drive a vehicle. We have made mistakes that have been our best life lessons to help us evolve. In all that time we've believed and not even realized that we have been doing it. We need to keep believing to allow life's process of us developing our wings. If we believe, it makes it easier to see.

Imagine we are our own movie producer. It's our story to tell and we know the storyline. Our characters are in place. We're in control of our own destiny. Our life depends on our self-image of ourselves. The more we can use our imagination to change and accept and believe our positive thoughts, and keep our positive attitude, we have the ability to change our self-image and become who we want to be. We can achieve our goals and set new ones. We need to keep raising the bar and imagine living the results. We need to keep focused and grateful for the pictures of the life we see, but live like it's already happening.

When we produce our movie, we already see the completed film. We surround ourselves with like-minded people who encourage each other and believe in us. Imagine dressing the part, talking the part, we need to live like that character in our movie. We'll change our thoughts which will change our actions and that will change our results. Our lives demonstrate where our thoughts and actions are because of the results we are achieving, so let's be a leader in our life.

I had come too far, down too many roads to turn back. I had a hard time all my life looking into that mirror and not loving the reflection I saw, but I was seeing the reflection others held for me. I wasn't who I believed I was. What I see is what I believe. I love myself and accept that I am a special, beautiful, smart, woman who can do anything. I'm strong and unstoppable. I am the person behind the wheel driving my own car toward my goal and I am so grateful that you came along for the ride and we shared our trip together. Go out and drive your car to your destination. Along your yellow brick road meet your Dorothy, Tin Man, Lion and Scarecrow. I'm so happy and grateful that you fastened your seat belt because it was a wild ride. Just because we reached our destination it doesn't mean that we can't make new ones. That's what it's all about. We'll see where the next adventure takes us. Imagine what your life will look like years from now.

Which character are you in the Wizard of Oz?

Can you imagine yourself playing the part of the person you want to be?

Are you ready to leave one luggage in your trunk?

What have you manifested in your life?

I AM WHO I AM.
I'M NOT THE PERSON YOU
THINK I SHOULD BE.

I'M NOT THE PERSON ANYONE ELSE
THINKS I SHOULD BE.

I AM THE PERSON'S REFLECTION
IN THE MIRROR WHO I SEE AND
THAT PERSON IS ME!

## ABOUT THE AUTHOR

Sandy Forseille was born in Enderby in the north Okanagan valley in British Columbia, Canada. Throughout her years she has accomplished many things, but her biggest accomplishment is the growth attained from her lessons. She's a strong woman who always wanted to prove to herself that she was good enough. Along her journey she's realized that it's about believing in herself and knowing her choices produced the results she achieved.

Sandy shares her personal stories to help others and wants to encourage her readers to remember that no matter our age, we can use our imagination. Our thoughts control our results, so if we desire different results, we need to change our thoughts and paradigms, replacing the negative ones with positive ones. We can accomplish what we desire if we believe in ourselves and just imagine.

10170814R00039

Manufactured by
Amazon.ca
Bolton, ON